There's
Magic
in the
Sky!

THE STORY **OF THE**
Aurora

SHANNA RUDOV-CLARK

Tales of Science and Magic
Dynnyrne, Tasmania 7005, Australia

2nd edition 2017

First published in 2016 by
Tales of Science and Magic in Australia

Pre-press by Forty South Publishing Pty Ltd
www.fortysouth.com.au

SUPPORTED BY

Tasmanian
Government

National Library of Australia Cataloguing-in-Publication entry:

Creator: Rudov-Clark, Shanna, author, illustrator.
Title: There's magic in the sky! : the story of the Aurora / written by
Shanna Rudov-Clark ;
illustrated by Shanna Rudov-Clark, Jasmine Kingsley,
Tegan Johnson, Linda Todd and Jarrod Leonard.

ISBN: 9780994495518 (Paperback)

Target Audience: For children.

Subjects: Auroras – Juvenile literature.

Other Creators/Contributors:
Kingsley, Jasmine, illustrator,
Johnson, Tegan, illustrator,
Todd, Linda, illustrator,
Leonard, Jarrod, illustrator.

Dewey Number: 538.768

To anyone who has looked up at the night sky and wondered.

When you travel up north
or way down to the south,
so you're nearer the north or south pole,

and you wander outside

on a clear and dark night

even though it is chilly and cold,

CONCEPTS
magnetic and
geographic poles

And then look north or south,

where the heavens meet earth,

well you might just be lucky and spy

a mysterious light –

maybe dim, maybe bright –

that is flickering up in the sky.

CONCEPTS
horizon

This magical scene may be yellow or green,

or purple or pink, red or white;

CONCEPTS
aurora beams
and curtains

it could look like a curtain that ripples and flows,

or beams reaching up in the night.

CONCEPTS
colours of the aurora

So enjoy this great show,

all the colour and glow,

don't be worried and don't be afraid;

we will tell you a story

and soon you will know

how we think this aurora is made.

It's a story, you see,

of a meeting between

the star that we like to call sun,

and a small lump of rock

that we like to call earth

where we all live

(except aliens).

Now, we know that the weight

of our planet is great

and it squeezes the

ground in the middle,

and we think

(we're not sure)

there's a big iron ball

that's surrounded

by hot runny metal.

CONCEPTS
composition of the
Earth's core

This liquid might churn,

as it rubs and it burns,

In a process that we call convection,

just like in a pot

full of water that's hot,

but this liquid has special reactions.

CONCEPTS
convection currents in the Earth's outer core

Some metals, you see,

make electricity

which form currents

that flow through our planet;

they are pushed by a force

as the earth spins around

into lines that create a big magnet.

CONCEPTS
The Earth's geomagnetic field

We will now leave this place
and we'll travel through space
to our very own sun – it's a star.
And while it seems pretty close
when it's burning your nose,
it is really incredibly far.

CONCEPTS
Solar System, distance between
the Earth and the Sun

See the sun is a mass

of some really hot gas

so big and so huge,

and we're told

that deep down in its centre,

there's way too much pressure,

which causes the gas to implode.

CONCEPTS
Hydrogen fusion

Everything that you see needs so much energy

just to stop it collapsing and burning,

and inside the sun all the energy there

can escape when the surface is churning.

CONCEPTS
solar storms

And the stuff that leaps out from this big ball of gas

is electrical, just like our iron;

it travels through space, at a speed close to light –

let me tell you, it really is flying.

CONCEPTS
coronal mass ejections,
speed of light

And when the wind blows,

eighteen hours or so,

it arrives at our very own planet,

to be caught in those lines between

south and north poles,

just like on a very big magnet.

CONCEPTS
solar wind,
the Earth's magnetic field

in patches of colour,

and the energy dancing

around in the sky

is the light that we call an aurora.

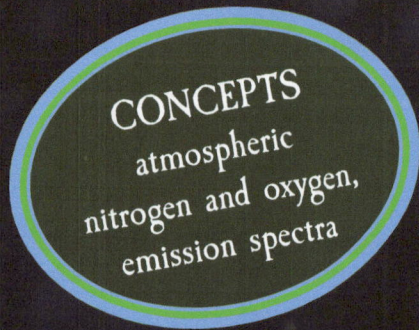

CONCEPTS
atmospheric
nitrogen and oxygen,
emission spectra

We hope you enjoyed our story.

This picture was taken

in Evandale, Tasmania …

isn't it beautiful?

Would you like to know more about the Aurora?

Do you have any questions?

You can visit us online at:

facebook.com/TalesOfScienceAndMagic

We'd love to chat with you

and show you some amazing pictures and videos.